Photography
Jan Chlebik
Len Grant
Paul Herrmann

MANCHESTER
THE MANCUNIAN WAY

Additional Photography
Ian Lawson

Edited by
Jane Price

CLINAMEN PRESS

Texts

No visitor to Manchester can fail to be captivated by its precocious energy. Its history is a chronicle of physical and intellectual manifestations of daring and innovation. From its pioneering days as the birthplace of the Industrial Revolution to its present day re-invention as an international gateway city of service industries in technology, communications, learning, sport and entertainment, it has shown enterprise, ambition and passion.

Its people are a compound of many nationalities and creeds emboldened by spirit of adventure, good humour and friendship. They are the products of global migrations and the city's unity today is its exciting diversity. They are entrepreneurial and pragmatic, unwilling to rest on past laurels and determined to match the achievements of history by sustaining an international city of the future.

They have much to live up to. The merchant venturers of the 18th century exploited Manchester's situation amid a flourishing textile boom to become the country's centre of production for cotton textiles. The tradition of global

FOREWORD: **DAVID PLOWRIGHT** ^{CBE}

THE RAINY CITY MYTH HAS BEEN EXPLODED

commerce continues and today embraces international links through finance and telecommunications. A labyrinth of canals were dug to provide transport and while some remain hidden beneath the city streets, others have been developed to provide a waterway setting for today's city living and café society.

The boldest act of the canal age was the building of the Manchester Ship Canal – opened in 1894 – linking the river Mersey with Manchester and making the city an ocean port. The canal was Manchester's response to high charges levied by Liverpool docks and its construction was one of the origins of the rivalry that exists between the two cities, now celebrated most noticeably in Premier League clashes between these two giants of English football. Manchester's strength was consolidated by the railway age; the line between Manchester and Liverpool, opened in 1830 was the first line between two large English cities.

The energy of these achievements was characteristic of Manchester's courage and sagacity. The city rapidly became a regional capital and major industrial, financial, commercial, shopping, educational and cultural centre. The huge warehouses that dominated the skyline and became decaying monuments to the city's industrial past are now being restored to provide the infrastructure of a modern 24-hour city.

There is still considerable architectural evidence of the city's past to be appreciated. The Town Hall is an ornate neo-Gothic structure designed by Alfred Waterhouse who also designed the main Manchester University

< Dusk over the River Irwell, showing The Lowry Hotel and Trinity Bridge alongside the Cathedral and Albert Bridge

∧ Urbis – Manchester's newest museum

Sandstone and steel at The Bridgewater Hall

Manchester's selection as the British candidate to bid for the 2000 Olympic Games although unsuccessful brought with it a new confidence to develop and sustain a major international city. The sporting achievements of Manchester United Football Club are legendary. The city's four universities form the largest learning campus in Europe; youth culture and popular music are pre-eminent; the arts and entertainment flourish and the city's streets resound to the rhythms of its many diverse festivals. The rainy city myth has been exploded and tourism is now a major contributor to the city's economy.

Hosting the 2002 Commonwealth Games is a privilege and serves as a tribute to the vision and determination of those resisting entrenched ideas and embracing the social and economic challenges of the future.

These pages illustrate our pride in what has been achieved.

buildings. Inside, wall paintings by Ford Maddox Brown depict the city's history. The John Rylands library built in the late Gothic style by Basil Champneys in 1899, the 15th century cathedral, and the Manchester Royal Exchange, an Italianate neo-classical structure built as a cotton exchange in 1874 and now home to the Royal Exchange Theatre Company, are all fine examples of our architectural heritage.

I came to Manchester in the late 1950s as a television journalist. In our craft we viewed Manchester with awesome respect because it was the home of *The Manchester Guardian* and its radical journalistic tradition of resisting the imposition of London's fashionable conventions on the rest of the nation.

This omniscience imbued those of us joining the infant Granada Television to take a similarly aggressive stand against London's natural tendency to dominate. Our mantra was that Britain speaking to Britain was a better prescription for a national broadcasting service than London speaking to Britain. Today's broadcasting industry faces new challenges from a multiplicity of new satellite and cable services but Granada has stuck to its Mancunian roots and absorbed many of its competitors. Its communications companions in the city are BBC North West and a number of successful independent producers.

During my time at Granada I kept a reporter's eye on those responsible for the social, political and cultural development of Manchester. The picture was not always rose coloured. Manchester struggled for some time with its management of change. But I came to admire the energy with which the City Council set about the modernisation of the city. Physical manifestations have mushroomed in the last two decades; The Bridgewater Hall, Manchester Art Gallery, the regeneration of the 1960s high-rise Hulme, The Lowry galleries and theatres, new hotels and housing, a revitalised commercial centre, and the stunning centrepiece for the 2002 Commonwealth Games – The City of Manchester Stadium – a personal satisfaction for me as a member of the design panel.

Waterhouse's Town Hall fills the three-sided plot of land earmarked in the 1850s. The commissioning town councillors were so aware of the importance of this building they ordered the structure be completed at any cost. The resulting neo-Gothic building is one of the finest of its kind

Manchester, the 2002 Commonwealth Games' host city, celebrates with the band James outside the Town Hall during the 1998 handover ceremony in Malaysia

if you use this city, you'll be spattered
with the drizzle of the elixir of youth

THE MANCUNIAN WAY

Market browsing

Attitude. Rain. Football. Music. Attitude. If you're not from round here, you probably know Manchester because of United, or Oasis or *Coronation Street*. In the case of Manchester United, it is worth remembering that, despite their huge popularity, and because of their global impact with competitive football, at least as many people in Manchester loathe them as love them. Knowing this, knowing that you make your way in the world drawing strength from fellow travellers, and not giving too much thought for the envy of rest, is what gives Manchester its attitude.

Vocal, direct, defiant, informal, hedonistic, unapologetic. Manchester is a new-world model, the product of its own invention. The first industrial suburb bred the industrial working class. This emergent group of non-indigenous city dwellers, who made their livings in the mills, workshops and warehouses of central Manchester, left real if ghostly marks, like shrimps in rock.

Attitude. Clannish, conservative, partisan. How else can you explain the way that the city continues to inhabit much the same street pattern, in many of the same ways that it has done since the middle of the 18th century? On Hilton Street in Manchester

TEXT: **PHIL GRIFFIN**   MANCHESTER IS PURE CITY, SMALL ENOUGH TO WALK, BIG ENOUGH TO BE LOST IN

city centre, barely 100 metres from Piccadilly Gardens, there are three-storey weavers' cottages with attic workshops and separate cellar addresses, whose tenants still trade in cloth and garments, more than 200 years on. Cities embrace continuity, tradition and homespun prejudice as much as rural communities. Across half a century, my school is in the same place, so is the hospital where I was born, the church where I was baptised, and my first-snog bus shelter. If cities are sculptures they are more, what Alexander Corder called, 'stabile' than mobile.

Cities find their optimum, usually by sprinting past it, and backing-up. North British cities have been depopulating for half a century. Today, there are signs of influx. Are gullible people simply putty in the hands of the marketing men when they sign-up for their 'lofts'? I don't think so. For years, city councillors and officers have twitched in the snares of listed building status. What to do with acres of unrentable

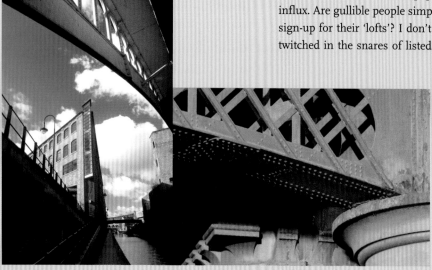

Castlefield, Britain's first
urban heritage park

Hindu wedding

grade II* Victorian warehouses? It was only after Lionel Richie sang "easy, like Sunday morning" in 1989, over a cool guy in Levi's in a Docklands loft, for a cash-card TV-ad, that we knew about 'lofts'. And Manchester was up for it. The city had the buildings, the singles, gay men and women, and developers waiting in the wings.

In 1960, Val Guest's film *Hell is a City* portrayed Manchester as a racy place, with flash-Harrys and floozys in back-alleys, boozers and snooker halls. Two years later, the Beatles sang *Love Me Do* on telly for the first time, in studio 4 of Granada TV, Quay Street. It helps, when the TV station on your doorstep challenges the Representation of the People Act and wins, is the first broadcaster on this side of the Atlantic to announce the assassination of JFK, and broadcasts the Sex Pistols' premier performance of *Anarchy in the UK*.

When something happens in a modern city, something is made of it. People write about it, or set it to music, photograph it or perform it. Manchester inspires novelists and poets, actors, stand-up comics, painters and video artists. There's a strong sense that the past can look after itself. It is the present and future tense that hold the moment. The people who are affecting Manchester are the people who are projecting it into the future. Sometime in the early 1960s, the intellectual centre of the city shifted from *The Manchester Guardian* to Granada TV, and it stayed there for nearly three decades. Today, it resides in the people who are driving the city's regeneration.

Manchester has never been a beautiful city. The Irwell, the Black River, was a dead thing by the time the Collegiate Church was elevated to Cathedral in 1847. Grand town houses soon gave way to warehouses when new banknotes were the issue. Manchester has no great river and no towering bluffs on which to site castles. The city grew pragmatically, and took a greater interest in economics than aesthetics. The mills and warehouses are efficient pieces of engineering. We worked in them, we shunned them, now we live in them. Manchester bristled with chimneys, that disappeared into the fog of their own making. Look up from street level today and see the Victorian Age as the Victorians never saw it.

We should be clear about what we have here. Not a beautiful city, but one that forges affection. Manchester has no signature view, no beach, no lake, no great gardens. But Manchester is pure city; small enough to walk, big enough to be lost in. Manchester's identity is set by the people who use the city, and who know how to love it for its rough good looks and easy virtue.

The coincidental century – the nineteenth – poses the great historical question, "Why? Why Manchester?" Why did a small inland town in south Lancashire come to dominate the world's trade in finished cotton goods, when the raw material did not exist within three thousand miles of the place? The coincidence of the Duke of Bridgewater's canals; the coincidence of coal and rotary steam engines; the coincidence of sewer building, tunnel cutting, track laying and the freight and passenger railways that led to the docks that serviced the ships that opened up the global market. The coincidence of nonconformity that created an anti-establishment of sectarian self-interest, that eased the flow of ideas, schemes and money. The chance meeting of people on the streets. The instinctive recognition of a fellow Manchester Man.

What have we got here? A community of hyperactive cityphiles, that knows how to love the whole place. You may have your Tivoli Gardens, Spanish Steps, Trevi Fountain, Golden Gate. We've got the neon blur of the Rusholme curry houses through rain-misted bus windows. We've got the giddy pavement promenade of under-dressed girls on Friday night, and excitable boys in Canal Street on Saturday. We've got pubs and clubs and bars, and we know how to use them. Baggy trousers, oversized tops, bikes and boards and BMWs with sound systems that could fill Old Trafford. And the *Royle Family*, Caroline Aherne's modern TV-masterpiece, of authentic and affectionate Wythenshawe council estate life.

New Manchester is about kids, and people who like kids. It's about living high on what you've got, and about making the city work for its people on their terms. You can take to the hills, if you like; stride the Lancashire fells above Bowland, or bathe in a hot orange Morecambe Bay sunset. You can internally digest your Wordsworth on Grasmere Common, swallow your territorial pride in a Yorkist castle, or survey Snowdonia from the Great Orme. Sure, you can do all of these things, and still be back in time for a sweaty night in a smoky bar, full of noise and beautiful girls and boys.

Manchester is about being young in a wicked city. And that is not exclusive. If you use this city, you'll be spattered with the drizzle of the elixir of youth. You will hang on, well into your fifties and sixties and keep company with other old hands who just can't let go. You'll see us most nights, eating crisps in licensed premises, looking for the next green light, hanging out in the first city of the modern world, looking forward, always looking forward, to tomorrow.

Beautiful countryside on the doorstep

I have a long association with the Mancunian Way. I studied art in its shadow, and two of my studios have overlooked it. At Hanover Mill it snaked right past my sixth floor window like a giant Scalextric set. I painted this view with its onrushing cars many times, by day and night

Liam Spencer

residents will be able to look out upon
the recreated city centre and contemplate
Manchester's transformation

CITY AT HOME

Terraces in Moss Side

Forget your images of LS Lowry and *Coronation Street*, we do not all live in little terraced houses. Around the city there are still leafy suburbs such as Didsbury and Whalley Range whence the middle-class population first moved in the nineteenth century away from the city centre. The country's first urban suburb, Victoria Park, commenced in 1837 – Queen Victoria's Coronation year – still has its magnificent villas, though too large for modern households and now much turned over to student halls. The workers' estates which sprang up around Victoria Park are now 'student villages'.

Of course, there is a legacy from our industrial past. Stretching like a girdle around the city were houses built to serve the myriad factories which drove Manchester's economic success. These were mostly not the back-to-backs so beloved of fiction writers, for Manchester banned these as early as 1844, but they were dreadful and overcrowded. Manchester's population growth in the nineteenth century was

TEXT: JOHN J PARKINSON-BAILEY

THE CITY IS BEING RECLAIMED FOR PEOPLE

unparalleled. Many of the terraces were cleared away in the post-war rebuilding programmes, but the buildings that replaced them were not wonderful, and when the industries closed they left great areas of economic depression.

But this is all changing. The City Council has generated major economic investment, not least through the staging of the 2002 Commonwealth Games, to revitalise and rebuild some of the poorest areas of the city. And public/private partnerships do work in Manchester. In Hulme there once stood the Crescents, named after Adam, Kent, Nash and Barry to evoke images of Bloomsbury and Bath; streets in the sky, built in the early 1970s to replace the awful Victorian

Adjacent neighbourhoods:
traditional homes and penthouse apartments

Community garden in North Manchester

slums. Built in a hurry and in materials little understood, the Crescents soon became a notorious place of muggers and vandals and vermin. In 1992, the City Council launched Hulme Regeneration with AMEC as private partners, and with architects to masterplan the redesign. 125 acres were cleared and rebuilt in five years. And now? Good quality social housing, private properties for sale and rent, architect-designed and tenant-led housing schemes, environmental improvements and new shops and jobs. Something for everyone, from first time buyers to student rentals; from single parents to families of all sizes.

Now, through Area Regeneration Partnerships, transformations are taking place in North and East Manchester, in Wythenshawe – England's third garden city – to the south, and in the area known as Eastside which stretches out from the city centre. Mixtures of new homes, improved houses, retailing and leisure, regeneration, sustainability. Even Ancoats – where slums stood cheek by jowl with those great palaces of industry, the late eighteenth century cotton mills which once turned more spindles than in the whole of Switzerland – is set to become an Urban Village. New uses for old buildings are being encouraged; residential and commercial use on the upper floors and retail, cultural and leisure uses on the ground floors to promote street activity.

And where, 150 years ago, people fled the city centre, they are now flocking back. In the 1960s the Lord Mayor was probably the city's only resident, and it was not until 1979 that the first small private housing estate was built near to the Granada Television studios. It was the same year in which Castlefield was designated a Conservation Area and regeneration began in earnest, and canal-side warehouses were reclaimed and converted into apartments. The site on which stood the Liverpool Road Station was transformed and became the Museum of Science and Industry in Manchester. These initiatives led to Castlefield being designated the country's first Urban Heritage Park in 1982.

On top of the Arndale Centre were 60 maisonettes and off Tib Street the Council built a small housing complex. It took another ten years before more schemes were developed: private and housing association apartments in converted textiles warehouses on Whitworth Street. Now, everywhere in the centre and beyond, Victorian warehouses, 1930s retail stores and even 1970s office blocks are being converted – mostly by Manchester architects – into apartments for DINKYs (dual

incomes, no kids, yet). The city's burgeoning service sector economy has created a need for educated, professional people and many of them choose to live in the centre. Manchester nowadays has a greater influx of residents than any other city in the UK. From a city centre population of less than one thousand in 1990, there will be some ten thousand inhabitants by 2005.

Manchester has already sold its first one million pound penthouse, the next one will be in a new-build on Deansgate. From its towering heights its residents will be able to look out upon the recreated city centre and contemplate Manchester's transformation from the cotton capital to a flourishing post-industrial city. For the first time in over a century and a half the city is being reclaimed for people and Manchester's regeneration can stand comparison with anywhere.

Restored alms houses in Heaton Mersey, now sheltered homes for the elderly

No. 1 Deansgate, designed by Ian Simpson Architects – Manchester's most prestigious address

Tower blocks in St Georges overlook the Mancunian Way

I was born in East Manchester on 28.3.1929. The Pit and the German Gasometer were the landmarks. Now it is the Stadium and the Velodrome. I have mainly worked in East Manchester, twelve years for Dr Brown, twelve years at the Probation Office and eight years with Victim Support. I know the people here and they are the best

Veronica Powell
Resident, East Manchester

Homes for Change, a unique scheme where tenant co-operatives drove the design of homes, shops, workplaces and communal facilities. Architects radically reinterpreted some features of the demolished deck-access housing at the tenants' request

Hulme and Moss Side, immediately south of the city centre, have, through redevelopment and rebuilding programmes, been transformed into vital and progressive neighbourhoods

<< As more people seek to live in the city centre, many developments are sold long before completion

< Granby House, the first conversion of an Edwardian warehouse into apartments

Smithfield Buildings in the Northern Quarter brought a new wave of design conscious dwellers into the city centre. Shops with meticulously designed apartments above have made this a desirable place in which to work and live

Once Manchester discovered loft living there was no turning back. The population within the city centre has more than doubled since the early 1990s bringing young professionals and families back into the heart of the city

>> Deansgate Quay, an eight-storey apartment block by Manchester architects Stephenson Bell overlooks the Bridgewater Canal

Doing it for themselves: once the engine room of a cotton spinning mill in Salford, designers Bill Campbell and Adrian Beaumont have converted the three storeys into a live/work space

From chic city centre lofts to high rise flats, people tune in to the world's longest running drama serial – *Coronation Street*

Unquestionably part of television history and a national treasure, Granada TV's story of the everyday lives of ordinary folk was created by Tony Warren and first transmitted on December 9th 1960

The show has been sold to 25 countries around the world, including Australia, Canada, New Zealand, South Africa, Estonia and Poland

CORONATION STREET

Images from the MEM@2K ongoing photography project which promotes understanding and awareness of Manchester's diverse ethnic communities. Clockwise from top right: Polish, Orthodox Jewish, Vietnamese, Pakistani

A large-scale project at the turn of the 19th century, Victoria Square, was designed to provide clean, 'moral' housing for one of the world's most intensely developed industrial centres. The five-storey building with its dramatic iron railings provided Manchester's first municipal housing. One hundred years on, Victoria Square still offers social housing to families and single people

Anita Street, adjacent to Victoria Square, was originally named Sanitary Street in honour of its improved water supply and sewerage system. Residents found the name distasteful and demanded its change

there's a word that keeps cropping up –
innovation. To achieve what it has in the latter
quarter of the twentieth century and to route
map the next fifty years, Manchester's people
have constantly innovated

INDUSTRIOUS REVOLUTIONS

The city's building boom continues

When I first came to Manchester, as a Londoner, 27 years ago I must say that I wondered what sort of place I was coming into. Its image had been cast as a dull and grimy city whose unique place in history, as the cradle of the Industrial Revolution, had long passed. The city is unrecognisable today and the transformation has been truly remarkable. When I look out of my twelfth-floor office windows at the pace and quality of the developments taking place, which show absolutely no sign of faltering, I marvel at the vibrancy of what is happening all around us.

The 150-year history of the Co-operative movement's headquarters here, established soon after its foundation just up the road in Rochdale, spans Manchester's period of glorious Victorian innovation to its exciting present day re-invention as a European regional capital and an international city of outstanding commercial, cultural and creative potential.

Our family of businesses, the Co-operative Insurance Society, the Co-operative Bank and the Co-operative Group, has thrived here – in a city now firmly established as the most important financial centre in the UK outside London.

We enjoy being involved with the prosperity of the city and its surrounding districts

TEXT: **SIR GRAHAM MELMOTH**   AN IMPRESSIVE RECORD OF INNOVATIVE RE-INVENTION

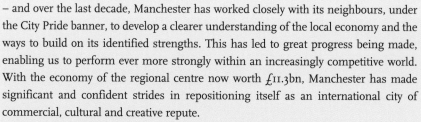

– and over the last decade, Manchester has worked closely with its neighbours, under the City Pride banner, to develop a clearer understanding of the local economy and the ways to build on its identified strengths. This has led to great progress being made, enabling us to perform ever more strongly within an increasingly competitive world. With the economy of the regional centre now worth £11.3bn, Manchester has made significant and confident strides in repositioning itself as an international city of commercial, cultural and creative repute.

This is not just Manchester's say-so. The alleged "rainy industrial city" plays host to huge numbers of visitors from within the UK and around the world who come here both to do business with the growing number of international companies based here, and to enjoy a unique cultural scene in the midst of a location within easy reach of some of Britain's prime countryside.

We are at the core of a wider Manchester city-region that has many clear areas of competitive advantage, not least one of the best regarded international airports in the world, now with a second runway, but also a recently completed orbital motorway and the UK's pioneering Metrolink light tram system with funding already in place to realise major extensions.

Manchester Airport voted by passengers as the world's best airport

Manchester – where rail travel began

The creation of Manchester Enterprises, as the economic development agency for the city, demonstrates the strength and capacity of the City Pride partnership to act effectively. This has been accompanied by the adoption of an agreed economic development plan setting measurable strategic goals.

Key to realising our vision has been the establishment of partnerships between local authorities, the business sector, government agencies and institutions of higher education. Manchester is a large city in many respects, capable of hosting the biggest multi-sports event ever staged in the UK – the Commonwealth Games – having provided the world-class facilities to do so. But the city is also small enough to enable all the major players, public and private, to focus on the achievement of common aims. We get on – and that's vital. This has fostered a can-do attitude towards the tasks that confront us, best illustrated by the dramatic way in which the city seized opportunity out of calamity after the devastating terrorist bomb attack which destroyed hundreds of businesses in the summer of 1996.

These relationships have given us a tremendous sense of get up and go; a model which others are trying to imitate. But they didn't of course, happen overnight. They grew over time, nurtured by the delivery of projects like G-Mex and the internationally-acclaimed new home of the Hallé, The Bridgewater Hall, to the provision of the city's latest showpieces like the International Convention Centre, now all supported by an unprecedented surge in hotel building to accommodate business visitors and tourists alike.

Against this background of co-operation, young entrepreneurs took considerable risks in converting what appeared to be unsalvageable relics from the Victorian era and pioneered the amazing boom in city centre living. Fresh innovative ideas for old buildings have also provided the means to house creative new enterprises, which feed from each other and flourish.

Significant infrastructure supports these developments, including TeleCity on Manchester Science Park, the only international internet exchange in the UK outside London. Forecasts for the coming ten years show impressive projected growth rates in several key sectors: computing services, communications, electronics, air transport and professional services. Investment sites include those in Manchester itself – the regional centre – in addition to developing clusters in neighbouring districts.

The higher education institutions – including four universities within two miles of Manchester city centre and a further 11 colleges across the wider area – have been particularly effective when working in partnership with local businesses. A key feature of this activity has been their increasing role, through research and development, in the creation of wealth and employment. This has been achieved through work to provide incubator facilities, particularly in the high technology sector and through public-private initiatives promoting creativity and entrepreneurship. The knowledge-based industries are now a fundamental part of Manchester's future.

Of course the universities also provide a regular flow of graduates in engineering, computing, industrial design and other technology-related disciplines upon whose skills the highest concentration of related industries outside the south east of England has become established. Some 30,000 people are employed in the software and computer servicing industry in the City Pride area and the surrounding region.

That Manchester is recognised as a good place to do business is underpinned by cultural strengths, from its iconic sports heritage, instantly identified in every corner of the globe, to its world-renowned musical tradition, both popular and classical, the vibrancy of its theatre and the treasures of its museum collections. These assets, from which spring a plethora of creative ideas, have seen phenomenal growth in recent years. The latest developments – Daniel Libeskind's stunning Imperial War Museum North in Trafford, the unique glass landmark of Urbis and the doubling of exhibition space at the Manchester Art Gallery – have maintained a remarkable momentum.

Both intensive business activity and burgeoning tourism, based upon our cultural diversity, account for Manchester having become the third most visited city in the UK. This is a phenomenon which may still raise eyebrows in the capital, but one that is underscored by the breathtaking growth in the retail sector as brand names of international prestige have jostled to set up shop in a centre not only enjoying a dramatic renaissance, but also, post-bomb, significant expansion.

Manchester's international roots run deep and are ever changing. We have been a welcoming people since the arrival of the Flemish Weavers in the Middle Ages, and our inclusive, enterprising spirit has, through Manchester Airport, a marvellous gateway for trade and communication with the rest of the world.

There is still much to do, but our determination to build on the achievements of what's already an impressive record of innovative re-invention, will be evident to every visitor.

Redundant buildings in Ancoats are revitalised by Carol Ainscow's Artisan H into combined work and living spaces

I joined the University of Manchester's School of Biological Sciences as a cell biologist. I am French and previously I worked in the USA. Like many scientists at the early stage of their career, I joined the University where the potential exists to become a world-class scientist. It's different from France – here there's more trust put in young people and there's the opportunity to really develop your scientific career

Dr Cathy Tournier

Manchester's much acclaimed Metrolink has brought trams back to the city's streets providing a popular means of transport while dramatically reducing peak-time road traffic

Well developed transport routes have always been of critical importance to the city's growth

Manchester Ship Canal in the 1880s created the world's first industrial city. Britain's first motorway was the Preston to Manchester section of what is now the M6. Today the city is at the hub of the most comprehensive system of roads and motorways in the country

The city centre lies twenty minutes from the third largest airport in the country, the only airport owned by the people – the people of Greater Manchester

Mancunians are not averse to attempting more novel modes of transport to get to places of work or play

< The remarkable curves of Gateway House snake up Station Approach towards a remodelled Piccadilly Station

∧ On the other side of the city, facing The Bridgewater Hall, new offices meet the demand from a burgeoning legal and financial services' sector

The city and its environs offer a superb range of hotel accommodation. The much loved Crowne Plaza Manchester – The Midland, known to Mancunians as simply 'The Midland', is a 1903 Edwardian building set in the heart of the city

Situated on the Salford-Manchester boundary is the five-star Lowry Hotel. Santiago Calatrava's Trinity Bridge across the River Irwell links the two cities

A day in the life of The Midland. Famous for its luxury and celebrated visitors – it was here that Mr Rolls met Mr Royce – it is the staff who maintain the reputation of this historic hotel. Servicing more than 300 rooms, international restaurants and beauty services, they keep the place running twenty-four hours a day

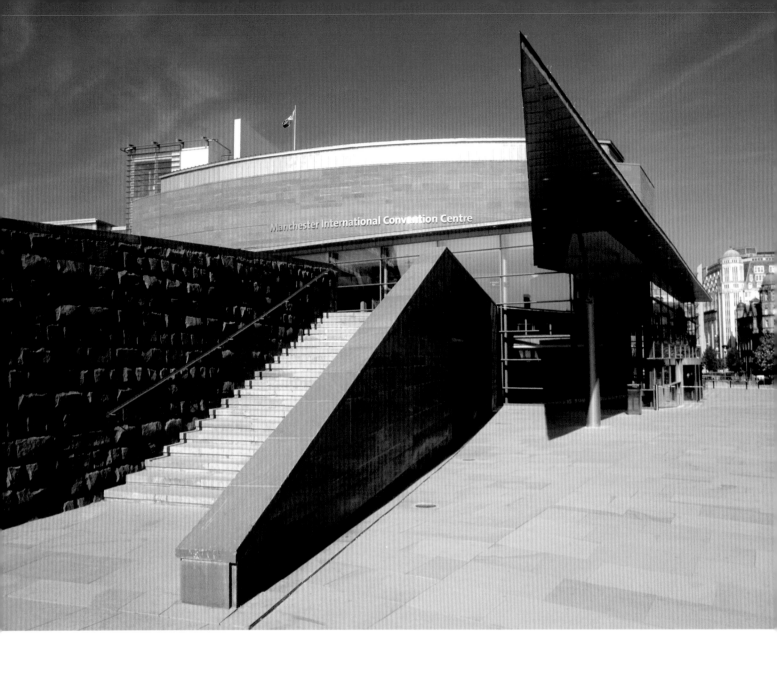

The recent opening of the £25m Manchester International Convention Centre, a state-of-the-art facility directly linked to G-Mex and adjacent to The Bridgewater Hall, creates a conference hub in Peter's Fields. Here also bars, restaurants and nightclubs lie alongside the Great Northern Experience, a huge leisure emporium

The Peterloo Massacre is commemorated also on this site and Manchester maintains its historic tradition of taking the people's voice to the streets. From the ancient Corn Laws protestors to modern day fair wage marchers, Mancunians continue to demonstrate their radicalism

>> Manchester's four universities, internationally renowned business school and music college have an annual intake of 70,000 students. The University of Manchester is the UK's preferred choice as a place in which to study a first degree

Communications industries have always had a powerful presence. Granada Television creates many of the nation's favourite programmes including the ever popular *Coronation Street*. BBC North West generates regional and national programmes for radio and television and Channel M, the country's first local terrestrial television channel, broadcasts daily

The Guardian newspaper, founded as *The Manchester Guardian* in 1821, dropped 'Manchester' from its title in 1959, moving printing to London in 1961. Its sister newspaper, the award-winning daily *Manchester Evening News*, frequently breaks stories that later become national news

< Cosgrove Hall, creator of many animated hits such as *Dangermouse* and *Chorlton and the Wheelies*, is the largest dedicated animation studio in the country

< 8.30 am and the first edition of the *Manchester Evening News* is put to bed

The city is a favourite location for film and television drama makers. *Cracker, Cold Feet* and *Queer As Folk* are among the most recent successes

> BBC Drama film *Cutting It* near Central Library

Sir William Siemens House, HQ for the
Automation and Drive Division of the blue-chip
company Siemens plc, is a striking landmark
for those entering the city by Princess Road.
With more than 2,433m² of glass, it's a
challenging job for cleaners

<< Traditional companies,
such as lifting and
mechanical handling
equipment
manufacturers Dale &
Company (Ancoats) Ltd,
have been trading here
since 1830

New media is the
foundation for the city's
explosion of
communications
companies, exemplified
by TeleCity, the
country's first internet
exchange outside
London

Manchester's textile manufacturing
industry continues to export clothing
throughout the world. This is Choudhary
Manufacturing Co Ltd in Ardwick

Since 2000,
Manchester Airport has
added a new terminal,
a second runway, two
hotels and a transport
interchange.
The continuing
expansion matches the
region's explosive
growth in tourism and
international business
with the Airport playing
a critical role

five years on, I still get a frisson when
I approach The Bridgewater and see silhouettes
drinking at bars on three levels

ART AND SOUL

Mark Elder conducts
the Hallé Orchestra

The Bridgewater Hall

Some time in 1995, I stood in the bare shell of The Bridgewater Hall, Manchester's newest concert hall, and looked up to the non-existent roof and tried to imagine the galaxy of twinkling lights I had seen on the plans.

As builders made their own kind of abstract music, I climbed on to the bare concrete slab that would eventually become the concert platform, stood roughly where a principal viola might eventually sit and gazed out past an unseen podium and conductor. Then I seemed to hear the sounds of things to come.

I know the Free Trade Hall, home to Manchester music (and politics) for almost 150 years, had a great history and tradition but I had come to hate it. Too fusty, too uncomfortable, too provincial. I couldn't wait for The Bridgewater to open, for Manchester to have a hall in which music-making and music-hearing would not be a penance. The first music I heard there in 1996 was Elgar's *Severn Suite*, played 20 times by contesting brass bands. When the impoverished and very unfancied Marple Band won in a Cinderella triumph, it seemed like a portent of unpredictable joys to come.

The Hallé, under Kent Nagano, marked the official opening with cool restraint. I made a personal attempt to liven things up by becoming the first man to attempt (by accident)

TEXT: **DAVID WARD**   CULTURE IN ITS BROADEST SENSE HAS, LIKE THOSE CAFÉ TABLES, TAKEN TO THE STREETS

to use the ladies' loos. Yan Pascal Tortelier, music director of the BBC Philharmonic, celebrated the occasion by bouncing around the radio and TV stations with irrepressible joy and directing a performance of Berlioz's enormous *Grande Messe des Morts* that must have featured every timpanist and brass player in the north. Strange, perhaps, to celebrate with a requiem. But as imaginative gestures go, it was a winner.

Barenboim came with the Chicago Symphony in that opening flourish and showed (with Tchaikovsky's Fifth Symphony) what the hall could do. Solti came, ruled the BBC Phil with a baton of iron, hobbled on to the platform, levitated on to the podium, turned to the audience and barked: "You haf a beautiful concert hall". Then he got on with the Shostakovich. Since then, Mark Elder has arrived as the Hallé's music director, has sought to place music in its historical, political and social context and has also frightened the wits out of everyone who heard his account of the last trump in Verdi's Requiem.

Five years on, I still get a frisson when I approach The Bridgewater and see silhouettes drinking at bars on three levels. The hall is a great people building, a welcoming village hall with immaculate white walls. And if the

Music student at
school band practice

music is boring, you can always count the twinkling lights. But I'm still not sure about the stair carpet. They tell me it was inspired by Monet's *Water Lilies*; I still say it looks like a bargain roll from Carpetworld.

For 20 years, not much happened in Manchester. There were glorious exceptions, of course. The Royal Exchange Theatre, with its in-the-round space capsule auditorium dropped into the pillared grandeur of the old Cotton Exchange, opened and people in the galleries found they were close enough to Tom Courtenay's head to check whether he had dandruff. The Cornerhouse opened too, with its galleries and two of its three cinemas converted from a furniture store. Patrons soon learned that if their chosen film was in the little auditorium buried somewhere downstairs towards the centre of the earth, the plot would be complex and the subtitles ample.

But sometime in the early 1990s, about the time someone said "to hell with the rain" and put the first bar table out on a Manchester pavement, things began to happen. Manchester decided that things did not have to stay the same. The city looked less to London and more to the world as it used to during the Industrial Revolution.

Then came the 1996 IRA bomb and Lottery money. I began to spend so long in a hard hat on arts building sites that I acquired my own. I was even photographed holding a bucket (I was supposed to look like a plasterer) in the lecture hall at the top of the Athenaeum while builders linked it forever to the spruced up and expanded City Art Gallery (or Manchester Art Gallery as we now know it) you see today.

The famous collection of pre-Raphaelite paintings have come out from the store, where they had waited with haughty impatience for the brickies to go away, and now hang on rosy-hued walls. Another old friend is back too: John Souch's *Sir Thomas Aston at the Deathbed of his Wife*, a hauntingly crude and beautiful portrait of the blackest of mourning. If things are going badly, I go and look at it and accept that things could be worse.

In the Lottery cash bonanza, both the loveable Octagon at Bolton and the Green Room under the arches in Whitworth Street West (where in the old days it could rain inside the auditorium) received cash injections – and then hit financial crises from which both have since recovered.

The Royal Exchange used Lottery funds to turn disaster into a triumph by repairing its bomb damage with the help of every scaffolding pole in Europe. The show had to go on, even if the building's three domes had been blasted up in the air and come down in the wrong places. So everyone decamped to Upper Campfield Market while the old hall was repaired and glammed up with pastel shades, pendulous lights and some alluring neon. Today the epic simplicity of the acting space remains unchanged, even if the hats and the furniture are sometimes better than the productions.

But the place that really hit the Lottery jackpot was The Lowry, the Salford Guggenheim built on a peninsula site down in the docks. It rose quickly, its stainless steel and glass reflected in Ship Canal waters which were not used to this kind of thing.

For weeks everyone talked about the colours (those purple walls!), the difficulty of finding the loos, the impossible car park (useful tip if you want to get out before midnight: pay in advance and do a Le Mans racing start as soon as the curtain comes down). Pensioners abandoned the Arndale Centre to spend happy days in The Lowry's warmth; other visitors poured in by the coachload. The Lowry pays its way with a careful mix of the posh and the popular and looks its best when stuffed with people.

The Lowry has helped us look seriously instead of adoringly or contemptuously at the work of LS Lowry and also does a fine wedding reception, when guests can toast the happy couple while watching the sun set over the Ship Canal. From its bars, we have been able to watch the rise of the jagged shapes of the Imperial War Museum North, which may prove to be the greatest building to be completed during Manchester's cultural boom. This is the first design by Daniel Libeskind, architect of the Jewish museum in Berlin, to be built in Britain.

The lovely old Palace Theatre and the Opera House have survived The Lowry's challenge with a mix of musicals and touring shows, and the Library Theatre, Britain's only municipally-run theatre company, beavers away in the basement of Central Library on St Peter's Square.

Manchester has changed. The Victorian city that supported art and culture because it did not want to be seen merely as a charmless centre of industrial wealth has gone on, like everyone else, to dither about the value of high culture and then decide that, on the whole, it is a Good Thing.

At the same time culture, in its broadest sense, has, like those café tables, taken to the streets with festivals, carnivals and gay Mardi Gras processions that stop the traffic in its tracks.

One enduring memory: a German company arrives in Castlefield to present its version of the Titanic story. The doomed ship is built and then sunk as dusk falls. More than 30,000 gallons of water are pumped from the canal and an actor clings for dear life as a mighty jet of water hits him up the rear end. The director later explains that the water pressure is far higher than anything they have experienced in Germany. Thus Manchester continues to develop its reputation for technological and artistic innovation.

Capturing the grandeur of Heaton Hall

As a practising artist, I handle works of art both in and out of work, so it's been a great experience working on the Manchester Art Gallery expansion project. It's inspiring to see more modern art on show: my favourite is Peter C by a certain Mr Hockney

Adam Quinn
Art Handling Technician
Manchester Art Gallery

Manchester Art Gallery has a new extension designed by architects Michael Hopkins & Partners. A £35m transformation doubles the space available for the internationally acclaimed art collection

A spacious new glass atrium links the new wing with the existing City Art Gallery and Athenaeum. These 19th century buildings have been cleaned and refurbished, restoring the beauty of the interior and exterior stonework

New galleries for permanent and special exhibitions, education studios, a shop and two café/restaurants make this an inspiring place to visit

Urbis is unique in design and content.
A museum of the modern city demonstrating the
history and experiences of people and
communities who have shaped urban spaces.
The four floors of exhibitions are imaginative and
interpretative combinations of audio, visual and
sensory environments

The glass-skinned building, designed by Ian
Simpson Architects, is set in Cathedral Gardens,
the Millennium Quarter's new green space

The Streets Ahead festival started in the mid-90s bringing street actors from around the world. X.trax in 2001 continued to excite audiences with art on the streets

Poetry, jazz, live music, food and drink all have their own festivals in a crowded entertainment calendar.

The gay and lesbian community celebrate with queerupnorth and Mardi Gras, the latter renamed Gayfest in 2001

The candle-lit vigil is at the heart of the four-day August gay celebration. Hundreds of revellers take time out from the festivities to remember friends and relatives who died from AIDS

Free festivals, open to all, bring art and culture to the most public of places – the streets, squares and parks. Mancunians love any excuse to party

Annual festivals celebrate the city's Asian, Chinese, Caribbean, Italian and Irish cultures. Mela and Diwali bring families in their thousands onto the streets of Rusholme and into the city's parks

Steel, glass and bold interior colours give Salford's The Lowry a majestic presence over the Manchester Ship Canal

Michael Wilford & Partners designed The Lowry which in 2001 won the Building of the Year Award from the Royal Fine Art Commision Trust

Inside are two theatres and numerous art galleries, one of which holds the largest collection of LS Lowry's paintings in the world

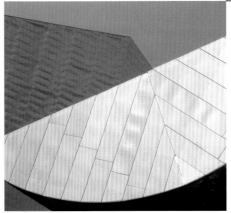

Intense colours in foyers and auditoria provide a warm contrast to the stark power of the building's steely exterior

Adjacent to The Lowry is Trafford's Imperial War Museum North, designed by acclaimed architect Daniel Libeskind. Its strong geometry and aluminium cladding create another powerful landmark within the regenerated docks

>> The Museum of Science and Industry in Manchester occupies the site of the world's first passenger railway station

>> Architecturally striking, the remodelled Contact Theatre is built around the 1960s auditorium

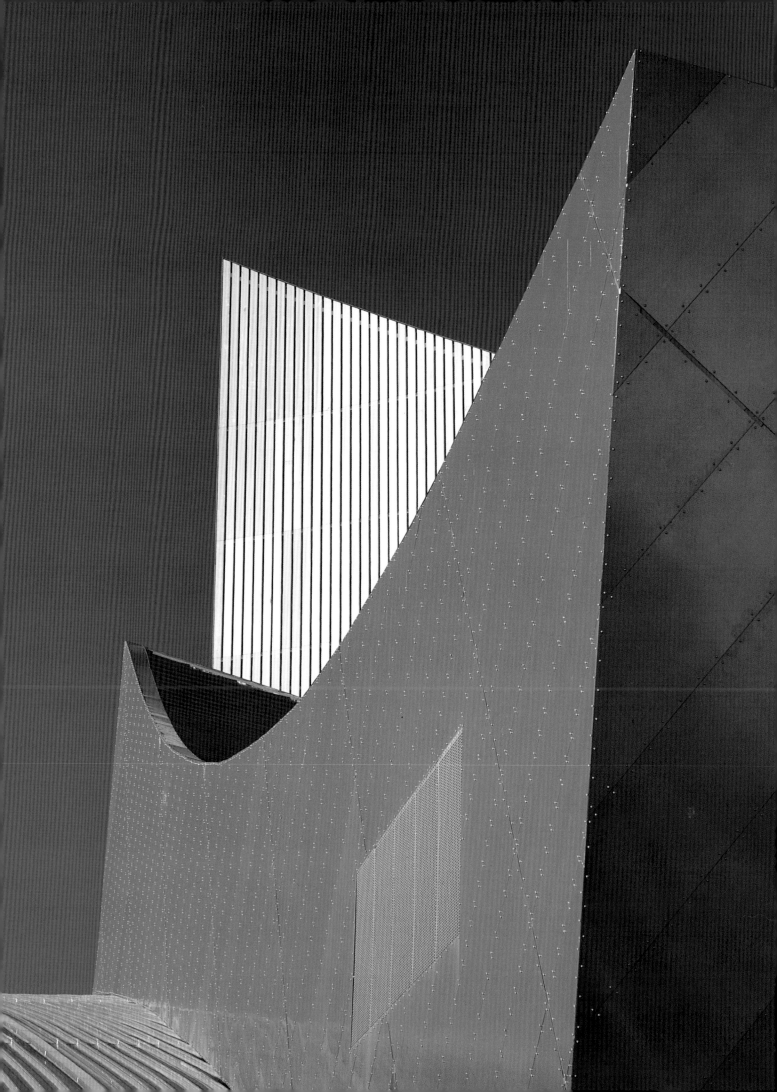

Vincent Harris's circular design of Central Library was inspired by the Pantheon in Rome. Opened in 1934, it has often been called the 'People's University' owing to its popularity as a library and as a meeting place. With more than 12 kms of shelving, it is the largest municipal library in Britain

The building combines literature with drama. In the basement is the Library Theatre, the UK's only municipally owned theatre company

Commemorative plaques mark the city's heritage and heroes

‹ Chetham's School and Library lie in the city's medieval quarter. Originally a boys' college in the early 1900s, it is now a distinguished mixed school of music. Chetham's Library houses the world's largest collection of books and pamphlets on the history of the north west. It was here that Marx and Engels met to discuss their politics and philosophies

The John Rylands Library on Deansgate, opened in 1899, was designed by Champneys and commissioned by Enriqueta August Rylands as a memorial to her husband, one of Manchester's great cotton magnates. The country's best stonemasons, woodcarvers and metalworkers were sought to craft this lavish building which houses the finest religious book collection in Britain

›› Manchester Cathedral is central to the city's new Millennium Quarter. Here visitors attend 'com.passion', a combined video, choral and music event

Performances in-the-round can be seen at the celebrated Royal Exchange Theatre. The central pod and building were remodelled after suffering extensive damage from an IRA bomb in 1996

At the height of Manchester's industrial prowess, the Royal Exchange was a thriving trading centre for textiles, cotton and other commodities

Mancunians are intensely proud of their
sporting pedigree and heritage, claiming the
title of Britain's Capital of Sport

SPORT CITY

The Manchester Velodrome

United fans celebrate... again

Manchester United. Two words that proclaim sport in Manchester to millions of people across the planet ... from Singapore to Surinam, Bombay to Boston. For Manchester United is more than just a football club, it is a sporting institution that has captured the headlines on the front and back pages of the world's press for almost half a century.

It may come as a surprise to learn, however, that once upon a time, mighty Manchester United was just Newton Heath, a football club founded by employees of the Lancashire and Yorkshire Railway Company and based in one of Manchester's less prepossessing suburbs. Formed in 1878, they won the Manchester Cup in 1886 and were elected to the Second Division of the Football League six years later. But in 1902 Newton Heath went bankrupt. The club was re-named Manchester United and in 1910, moved across the city to Old Trafford, already the home of Lancashire County Cricket Club.

A sporting dynasty was born, and since emerging from the trauma of the Munich air disaster in 1958, in which 21 people, including eight players, perished, Manchester United has brought the city a worldwide recognition that is shared by only a handful of elite clubs. Real Madrid and New York Yankees are up there with them in the Pantheon. But not many more.

TEXT: **ANDREW COLLOMOSSE**   A ONCE IN A LIFETIME OPPORTUNITY TO BECOME THE DE FACTO CAPITAL OF UK SPORT

For a lot of people born and bred in Manchester, though, the red shirts of United will always play second fiddle to the light blue of Manchester City. More than 30,000 devoted supporters follow City through thick and thin. And apart from an occasional glimpse of the sunshine beyond the giant shadow of Old Trafford, times have been decidedly thin for the last 50 years or so, prompting the Maine Road faithful to mine a rich seam of self-deprecatory gallows humour.

You know the kind of thing: "A friend of mine asked his lad what he wanted for Christmas. He replied, 'a cowboy outfit'. So my pal went out and bought him Manchester City." Yet the light blue cognoscenti proudly assure us that, unlike that cosmopolitan lot up the road who wear suits on match days and speak with southern accents, their supporters actually hail from Manchester.

Mammoth hoarding promotes the Commonwealth Games

My first experience of City supporters was visited upon me at Leeds Road, Huddersfield, on September 9, 1953 and nothing that has happened in the intervening years has altered my original view that they are a rum lot.

In those days, no-one bothered about segregating rival fans on the simple, if now naive, precept that people paid good money to watch a game of football rather than indulge in 90 minutes of tribalistic threatening behaviour. And so it was that my Dad and I found ourselves surrounded by a large group of men sporting light blue and white scarves, smelling of ale and turning the air a darker shade than their team's shirts with language deemed highly unsuitable for my sensitive seven-year-old ears.

The inevitable paternal protest followed and profuse apologies were offered along with a non-stop supply of Cadbury's mis-shapes. Not another oath was uttered all afternoon and at the end of the game (the record books say it was a 1-1 draw) one of the City fans handed me the remains of the mis-shapes, saying: "Here sonny, you might as well have 'em. I can't stand chocolate." As I say, a rum lot.

The Lancashire cricketing fraternity can be a singular bunch too. The Red Rose county has been up and running since 1864, won the County Championship eight times and collected 16 trophies in one-day competitions. Some of the most momentous Test matches in the history of the game have been staged at Old Trafford. And one way to sample the level of intensity in sporting Manchester is to find a seat in the Old Trafford pavilion during a Roses Match against Yorkshire.

There was a time, immortalised in the writings of Neville Cardus, when the County Championship Battle of the Roses would attract a near 30,000 full house on each of its three days. The strict edict was no fours before lunch on the first morning as these deadliest of sporting rivals jockeyed for position in the battle to avoid defeat. These days the crowds have all gone home as far as Championship Cricket is concerned but you still won't find many more passionate environments than the Lancashire members' enclosure during a one-day semi-final against the White Rose.

However, there is far, far more to sport in Manchester than a couple of soccer teams and a cricketing institution. For Manchester is truly united in sport. Greater Manchester boasts eight professional football clubs, a host of non-league teams, four Rugby League clubs including Wigan, the 13-a-side code's equivalent of Manchester United, and Sale Sharks play in Rugby Union's Premiership. Athletics? How about Sale Harriers, one of the country's leading clubs. The opportunities for amateur sportsmen and women are endless.

Think of a sport ... and you can find it in Manchester, whether you're a participant or a spectator. Mancunians are intensely proud of their sporting pedigree and heritage, claiming the title of Britain's Capital of Sport. Suggest otherwise and it could be the end of a beautiful friendship.

Until now, though, it has been an unconvincing argument, despite Manchester playing host to several world-class events in recent years. You could have made out an equally strong case for London, Birmingham or Glasgow, which, like Manchester, have staged their share of international competitions and have their heroes and heritage too. Sheffield, Edinburgh, Newcastle, Cardiff and Leeds have not been a million miles behind, either. Until now...

For the year 2002 and the XVII Commonwealth Games changed all that. Manchester City Council has been chasing the big one for some time; a major sporting occasion that would focus global attention on the city and prove to the world that Manchester, and Britain for that matter, could host a genuine world-class event. After two unsuccessful Olympic bids, the Commonwealth Council for England chose Manchester as their city ahead of London and Sheffield; the Commonwealth Games Federation gave the green light and it was all systems go.

Manchester 2002 features more than 5,000 competitors from 72 nations competing in 17 sports in a series of world-class venues. The City of Manchester Stadium, Manchester City Football Club's new home from 2003, towers above Sportcity, a complex that also features the National Cycling Centre, the National Squash Centre and an Indoor Tennis Centre. The Belle Vue Regional Hockey Centre is just down the road with the Manchester Aquatics Centre's Olympic-class facilities not far away. These new world-class venues represent the most significant sports investment this country has ever undertaken and, crucial to the city's plan, they provide the catalyst for regeneration in East Manchester.

The Bolton Arena is already established as a Regional Centre of Excellence for the Lawn Tennis Association and Heaton Park, on the outskirts of the city, now has a state-of-the-art Lawn Bowls complex – another new Centre of Excellence. Manchester also boasts a top-class Triathlon course, based around the futuristic Salford Quays, and front-line indoor venues in G-Mex and the Manchester Evening News Arena.

All these facilities will serve the region long after the XVII Commonwealth Games has been consigned to the history books. Such world-class venues will enable Manchester to stage major events for years to come. They also provide top-class training and fitness facilities for elite athletes of all ages and they are there for the people of Manchester and the Northwest region too. The face of Manchester sport is about to change forever.

Inevitably there has been opposition. Providing facilities of this stature is a costly business even with major National Lottery funding from Sport England. Like it or not, that's progress. We can't have it both ways. It's no good bleating about British sport falling behind our major rivals and then complaining when a city like Manchester takes the bull by the horns and does something about it.

With work on Manchester's new stadium completed while London still waits to build a national stadium, and the capital's bid to stage the 2005 World Athletics Championships a non-starter, the 2002 Commonwealth Games has given Manchester a once-in-a-lifetime opportunity to become the de facto capital of UK sport and one of the world's pre-eminent sporting cities.

Shaolin Kung Fu at Wythenshawe Leisure Centre

It all began in November 1995 with a visit to the Manchester Velodrome. I had gone along to an induction session to see what all the fuss was about. It took that one session and I was hooked. I immediately began racing on Friday night track leagues, driving down after work from Lancaster in my girlfriend's mini metro. As they say the rest is history, in September 2000, I became an Olympic Champion in the one kilometre time trial. Quite simply if the Velodrome had not been built in Manchester I would have not have been an Olympic Champion

Jason Queally

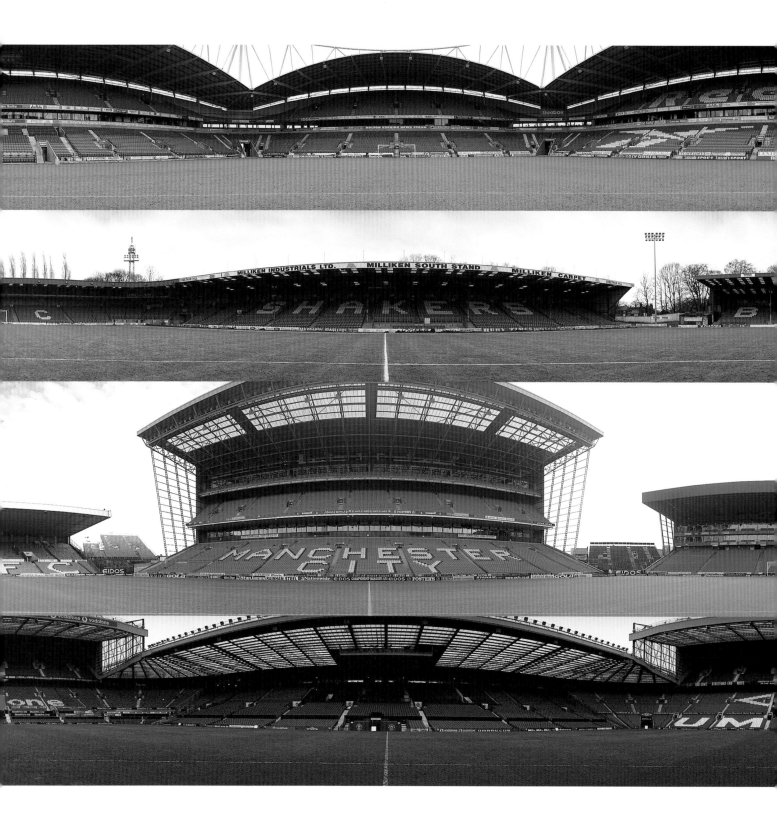

BOLTON WANDERERS FC   Club nickname: The Trotters   Ground: Reebok Stadium   Ground capacity: 27,879   Record attendance: 69,012 v Manchester City, FA Cup, 5th rd, 18 February 1933   Year formed: 1874 | BURY FC   Club nickname: Shakers   Ground: Gigg Lane   Ground capacity: 11,669   Record attendance: 35,000 v Bolton Wanderers, FA Cup 3rd rd, 9 January 1960   Year formed: 1885 | MANCHESTER CITY FC   Club nickname: Blues or The Citizens   Ground: Maine Road   Ground capacity: 34,026   Record attendance: 84,569 v Stoke City, FA Cup 6th rd, 3 March 1934 (British record for any game outside London or Glasgow)   From 2003 – City of Manchester Stadium   Ground capacity: 48,000   Year Formed: 1887 as Ardwick FC; 1894 as Manchester City | MANCHESTER UNITED FC   Club nickname: Red Devils   Ground: Old Trafford   Ground capacity: 68,174   Record attendance: 76,962 Wolverhampton Wanderers v Grimsby Town, FA Cup semi-final, 15 March 1939   Year formed: 1878 as Newton Heath; 1902 as Manchester United

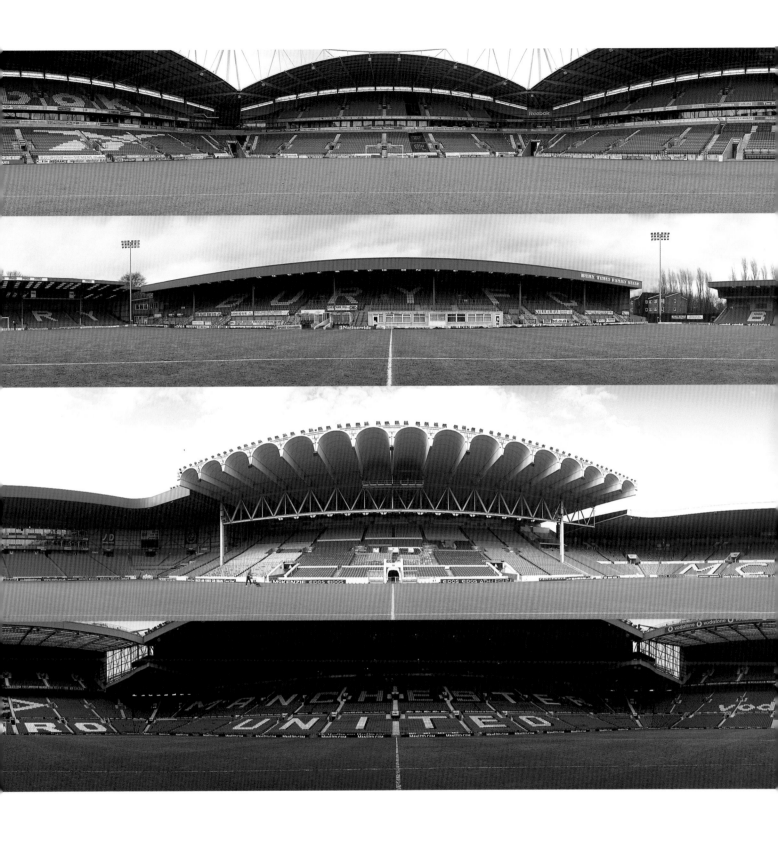

OLDHAM ATHLETIC FC Club nickname: The Latics Ground: Boundary Park Ground capacity: 13,559 Record attendance: 47,671 v Sheffield Wednesday, FA Cup 4th rd, 25 January 1930 Year formed: 1895 | ROCHDALE FC Club nickname: The Dale Ground: Spotland Ground capacity: 10,249 Record attendance: 24,231 v Notts County, FA Cup 2nd rd, 10 December 1949 Year formed: 1907 | STOCKPORT COUNTY FC Club nickname: County or Hatters Ground: Edgeley Park Ground capacity: 11,541 Record attendance: 27,833 v Liverpool, FA Cup 5th rd, 11 February 1950 Year formed: 1883 | WIGAN ATHLETIC FC Club nickname: The Latics Ground: JJB Stadium Ground capacity: 25,000 Record attendance: 27,526 v Hereford Utd, 12 December 1953 Year formed: 1932

<< Belle Vue, once home to a zoo, has 'gone to the dogs' at the popular Belle Vue Greyhound Track

The sixth Manchester Marathon adopted a new route as a road test for the 2002 Commonwealth Games. For the first time, 1500 competitors ran along Deansgate in the heart of the city centre

Continuing the Club's phenomenal success, more than half a million supporters took to the streets to celebrate Manchester United's historic triumph in 1999 when the team won the Premiership, the European Champions' League Cup and the Football Association Cup

The hallowed cricket ground at Old Trafford where Lancashire County Cricket Club played their first match in 1865

Sunday sport: amateur cyclists from Manchester clubs meet while elite athletes limber up for the Salford Triathlon

The Manchester Aquatics Centre is the only complex in Britain with two 50-metre pools. The eight-lane ground level pool is used by local swimmers and national and regional competitors. Flumes, chutes and whirlpools add to visitors' enjoyment while a separate 25-metre diving pool features one and three metre springboards and a ten metre highboard. A four-lane pool on the lower level is used by swimmers training for international and national competitions

Built in time for the 2002 Commonwealth Games, the Manchester Aquatics Centre provides the city with a lasting benefit from hosting the Games

City of Manchester Stadium: the catalyst for regenerating East Manchester

Sportcity is the UK's largest investment in sport to date. At the heart of the complex is the City of Manchester Stadium which has transformed for ever the city's skyline. Seating for 38,000 spectators at the 2002 Commonwealth Games will increase to 48,000 before Manchester City Football Club adopt the stadium as their new ground in 2003. Alongside is the new National Squash Centre, an athletics arena and an outdoor athletics track

Sportcity under construction – November 2001

I suppose it all began with a chipped teapot on a wipe-clean Formica-topped table...

CONSUMING PASSIONS

Hodder Associates' footbridge
over Corporation Street

I suppose it all began with a chipped teapot on a wipe-clean Formica-topped table...
Not the most obvious start to a revolution, but with more than 30 years of hindsight, it really was Manchester's first ingredient in the remarkable recipe that served up the finest and most diverse restaurant culture of anywhere in Britain outside the capital.

There had been one or two Chinese restaurants in the city before the opening of the original Kwok Man in the late 1960s, a completely unsung event in a corner of an inauspicious Victorian building, long demolished, but it was here Mancunians first encountered the true taste of authentic Hong Kong Cantonese cuisine. And they loved it.

From such humble beginnings sprang Manchester's Chinatown, as first one, then another enterprise opened to meet a burgeoning appetite. The square mile to the south of Piccadilly, once threatened with being razed to make way for the modern concrete development that epitomises the Plaza, instead took on the unique, successful and exciting cultural character we see today. The erection of the ornately beautiful Chinese arch in the heart of the quarter, sealed its recognition by European and Oriental Mancunians alike.

TEXT: **RAY KING**

PREVAILING SPIRIT DECREED THAT DISASTER SHOULD SPAWN OPPORTUNITY

In the 21st Century, Chinatown is the first culinary stop for visitors to the city and, in the Yang Sing, Manchester boasts by national critical acclaim, the finest Chinese restaurant west of the Great Wall.

But the dining-out revolution sparked here was not confined to the thriving scene around the pagoda arch. The very nature of great Chinese cooking requires the best and freshest of ingredients. The scale of that requirement galvanised markets and suppliers, and not just to serve the Thai, Malaysian, Japanese and especially Indian sub-continental restaurants that have multiplied around the city.

Manchester not only boasts its Chinatown, but a 'Little India' too, with more than 50 restaurants, cafés and sweet centres serving Punjabi, Bengali, Kashmiri, Persian and Nepalese food and forming the largest single concentration of Asian cuisine in Britain. The 'Strip', a mile and a half outside the city centre in Rusholme, is a brash and vibrant, neon-lit slice of intoxicating cultural life visited by 10,000 people a week.

These modestly priced ethnic restaurants triggered a major shift in Mancunian lifestyle. They made the habit of eating out among locals as commonplace as going to the pub. The humorist Alan Bennett's reminiscences sum up perfectly the social agonies many ordinary

The Old Wellington Inn and
Sinclair's Oyster Bar

Vivienne Westwood greets '*Corrie*' star John Savident
at the opening of her Manchester shop

northern folk would endure, even in a humble café, whether ordering eggs on toast or potato croquettes at the Kardomah, let alone if they ever found themselves amid the formal magnificence of the French Restaurant at the Midland Hotel. They never would, of course, for dining there was what posh people did.

The French was for decades a solitary beacon of haute cuisine. But cometh the men, cometh the revolution in the wake of the innovative, design-led explosion that saw Manchester's club and bar culture become the envy of not just Britain, but the world.

Paul Heathcote, young Boltonian protégé of the great Raymond Blanc was the first of the young 'celebrity chefs' to establish in Manchester after winning two coveted Michelin stars at his first solo venture in the Lancashire hills. His was a pioneering fusion of modern British cooking and radical contemporary restaurant design, following which some of the most famous names in resurgent British cooking have followed suit in an unprecedented stampede to reap the fortunes of a booming city.

Blanc himself took personal charge of his striking Manchester enterprise. Sir Terence Conran set up his first venture outside London and Marco Pierre White masterminded the formula at the MPW River Room at Sir Rocco Forte's new five-star Lowry Hotel on the Salford bank of the River Irwell. Gary Rhodes has now lent his signature to the restaurant at the Thistle Hotel, Manchester, in addition to Rhodes & Co in the shadow of Manchester United's 'Theatre of Dreams' at Old Trafford.

These developments are not simply lifestyle side shows but key to the emergence of Manchester as a major player on the European stage, recognised and used in evidence by none other than the Iron Lady, Margaret Thatcher herself. Challenged on one visit to the city about the alleged north-south divide, the then prime minister reached for *The Good Food Guide*.

The winds of change, enthusiastically embraced, that ushered in the transformation of Manchester's reputation for restaurants were even more dramatic in establishing one of Britain's most dynamic shopping meccas. In six short years of astonishing developments, triumph has emerged from potential disaster.

Shortly after 11am on 15 June 1996, much of the commercial and retail heart of the city centre was in ruins. The largest bomb ever to explode on the British mainland in peacetime had laid waste to hundreds of businesses, large and small, national and local. The Arndale Centre, when built, the largest undercover retail mall in Europe, loved by shoppers if not by architectural aesthetes, suffered grievous damage. Opposite, one of the busiest Marks & Spencer stores in the UK was shattered beyond repair. Worse still, the calamity happened just as Manchester city centre was about to face its most serious competition ever, a million square feet of brand new retail space at the Trafford Centre, five miles away.

The city was faced with a race for its life and against time. But the prevailing spirit decreed that disaster should spawn opportunity; the city would be bigger, better; and so it has proved.

Even before the explosion, change had been taking place. The programme of rebuilding and with it, remarkable expansion, instituted an astounding change of gear. Best of all, the in pouring of the new went hand-in-hand with the preservation of Manchester's rich Victorian heritage.

As pledged, a rebuilt Marks & Spencer rose from the ruins; a modern glass sheathed landmark now shared with Selfridges. The master plan opened up a new square paving the way for the old Corn Exchange to exchange its status from decaying home of a flea market to The Triangle, a brilliantly conceived galleried three-level centre for specialist designer stores beneath its restored soaring glass domes. Opportunity was also seized to rid the city of an eyesore concrete precinct nearby and a modern replacement includes luxury apartments. Here, also, Harvey Nichols is boosting the already impressive roll call of benchmarked quality.

As with The Triangle, opportunity knocked for a relic of Manchester's industrial legacy when the former newspaper plant opposite was accorded ingenious, multi-million pound rebirth as The Printworks, a leisure complex with a capacity for entertaining 25,000 people 24 hours a day.

It stands like a bookend at one side of the compact city centre with the rapidly developing Great Northern Experience, the metamorphosis of a gigantic Victorian railway warehouse, on the other. In between, the elegant halls of Manchester's commercial heart have been colonised by world famous names like Armani, Calvin Klein, DKNY and Diesel in an emphatic demonstration of international confidence.

Amid these icons to fashion and the multitude of pavement cafés, giving lie to the city's rainy reputation, Mancunians strut with a spring in their step knowing there is still more, much more, to come.

Why Manchester? Easy, I was born here, in Crumpsall Hospital, 2 Ken & Gloria... Higher Ardwick from Jamaica 2 Manchester, 1 of the more tolerant cities in England. Playing music & business take me away from 0161 and what you miss R Community & Vibe. It is a misconception that all Manchester has 2 offer is the music scene & football. 2 me people stay here because of the people who add energy 2 the city. If U were 2 ask many of the people who move here, why they choose Manchester the reply would be Community makes Manchester so special

Elvis Oakley
Afrosaxon, Afflecks Palace

Manchester's shops offer style and diversity to
match any budget and any taste. From
international designer labels to high street stores,
with more than 500 outlets, it's a shopper's heaven

The Millennium Quarter also embraces Chetham's School and Library; the Cathedral; Urbis; Sinclair's Oyster Bar and Old Wellington Inn and a new park, uniting this historic area with the rest of the city centre

The Triangle, with its upmarket shops and restaurants, was once the Corn Exchange. This 1897 building is part of the Millennium Quarter which includes Exchange Square, a new public space designed by Martha Schwartz as part of this area's regeneration following the 1996 IRA bombing

Marks and Spencer's store and Selfridges face onto the square, which is really a triangular space, as does The Printworks, an entertainment mecca with its many bars, nightclubs and restaurants

Embracing café culture and taking to the streets to eat, whether it is at café bars or traditional 'chippies'

There are more than 500 bars and restaurants serving cuisine from over 30 different countries. Manchester has more entries in *The Good Food Guide* than any other city outside the capital

TEXT: **CATH STAINCLIFFE**

Beyond here stretch the northern territories, poor, flat lands running up to the hills of Oldham and Rochdale. The wrong side of the tracks. Northern Quarter – time was this was a sorry place; neglected, low rents, vacant lets. The warren of streets and crumbling buildings offered a whiff of opportunity to entrepreneurs, specialists, idealists, fanatics, desperadoes, collectors, rebels, pioneers. Risky business. Fashionable now. The edge of town, spitting distance. Des res. Though there's still an edge.

Fun fur by the pound at Abakhan's, or silk or muslin, chintz and calico. Buy your bits for Mardi Gras, the school play, that duvet set, the bridesmaids, Hallowe'en, the baby's room. Plonk it in the scales. Down the road's the rag trade, in every window this season's styles and outside people loading vans, carrying armfuls of garments sheathed in plastic.

Lots of independent shops. No chains here, well not that sort. Can do you nipple chains, chain-mail, chains of circumstance, Chain of Fools. Sometimes, sadly, chains of evidence.

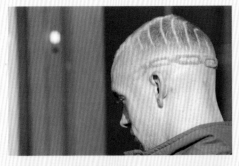

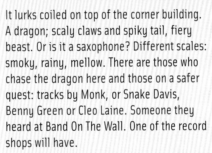

Here be aliens, robots and daleks. Not full size – though there's an original in Affleck's that triggers the thrill of terror down the spine and the memory (for the *Dr Who* generation) of watching from behind the sofa. Did we really think we were safe there?

It lurks coiled on top of the corner building. A dragon; scaly claws and spiky tail, fiery beast. Or is it a saxophone? Different scales: smoky, rainy, mellow. There are those who chase the dragon here and those on a safer quest: tracks by Monk, or Snake Davis, Benny Green or Cleo Laine. Someone they heard at Band On The Wall. One of the record shops will have.

 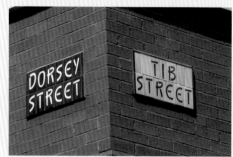

Years back, late at night, the light sang out from the Daily Express building on Great Ancoats street, curved ribs of black, plates of glass, art deco. You could see the papers rolling off the presses, like something out of *Citizen Kane*.

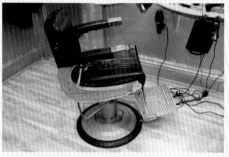

on Tib Street
look beneath your feet
poetry
stepping stones poems
metres apart metres that start
changing the rhythm
of the way you walk
pavement
talking the talk
on Tib Street

 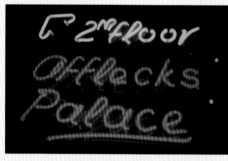

  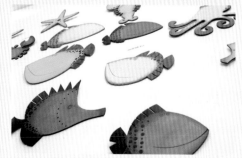

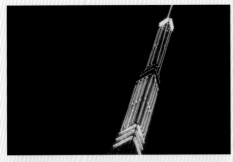

Time was they tried to close Affleck's Palace,
regulate it as a market, eviction in the air, the
traders won the fight ... thriving now.
First rate experience second hand bargains
third world music fourth dimension.
A bizarre bazaar, a cornucopia of delights and
little shocks.

TEXT: **CATH STAINCLIFFE**

Tib Street housed the pet shops and the joke
shop. Building The Bridgewater Hall they found
rare water snakes in a culvert. Reckoned they'd
escaped from Tib Street and were breeding
beneath the city. We used to go to the joke
shop for stuff for the playschemes, and had
lunch round the corner in The Yacoub.
Authentic style, use the chappattis to scoop up
your curry, feel the tingle on your lips for the
rest of the afternoon.

< Deliveries arrive early in the morning as Chinatown prepares for a busy day

Since the 1970s, Manchester's Chinatown has established itself as the largest Chinese community outside of London. Here banks, medicine shops, financial and legal services operate alongside a wealth of restaurants and supermarkets

∧ The Yang Sing Restaurant on Princess Street is an institution, consistently producing the best Cantonese food in Britain

>> Gulab Jamun simmering in the Sanam Sweet House and Restaurant in Rusholme's 'curry mile'

Traditional bartering and bargain hunting can be had at many of the city's markets. From fruit 'n' veg to fish; from bric-a-brac to antiques; Farmer's and European Markets; indoor and outdoor, there's nothing that can't be picked up

it's not always possible to know exactly what's going on, but in Manchester you can always be sure that something is going on

DUSK TO DAWN

it's not always possible to know exactly what's going on, but in Manchester you can always be sure that something is going on

Barça restaurant in Castlefield

I was DJ-ing, live for a radio station, broadcasting from the window of the Oxfam shop on Oldham Street, in the midst of the Northern Quarter. Here the city hosts many of the most successful enterprises of the post-Haçienda generation; record shops and record labels, club promoters, magazine offices, designers. It's a part of the city where creativity and commerce meet, and where urban tensions are tangible.

It was one of Oldham Street's quieter nights, a melancholic mid-evening under a leaden sky. I played a rare soul classic from America, *Harlem Shuffle* by Bob & Earl, a crackling old 7" record that clubbers would have travelled miles to hear in 1965, well before superstar DJs, New Order, the Haçienda. The record felt very powerful. The music was unlocking something in the city. Although the pavement outside was cold, wet, and empty, I felt the presence of ghosts, generations who'd queued,

TEXT: **DAVE HASLAM**   THE MUSIC WAS CONNECTING ME, THEM, THE PAST AND THE FUTURE

danced, got off on the music. It was eerie. The music was connecting me, them, the past and the future.

The story of how pop culture has reflected and shaped life in Manchester goes back decades. I remember a slogan you used to see scrawled on walls in the late-1970s: "no future". The manufacturing industries that had given cities like Manchester, Liverpool and Birmingham a powerful place in the world economy 150 years ago had finally collapsed, leaving a legacy of derelict warehouses and factories. In Manchester, Oldham Street – once the major shopping street of the city – had fallen into disrepair. All around, LS Lowry meets *Bladerunner*.

The Printworks, once the site of the largest newspaper printing works in Britain, now a popular entertainment centre

Punk was a response to this chaos and a way out of it. Manchester bands like The Fall, Magazine, and Joy Division unshackled punk from two chord thrash and bondage clichés and independent record labels like Rabid, New Hormones, and then Factory emerged out of this whirl of post-punk activity. Factory began to have success, especially with New Order.

In 1982 Factory Records and New Order opened the Haçienda in an old warehouse on Whitworth Street West, in what was then just another decrepit part of Manchester. The club never made money. Although I don't quite believe him, New Order's bass player, Peter Hook, claims that instead of opening the club they'd have been better off giving each of the thousands of people who'd ever queued outside £10 and told them to go home. If the Haçienda cost New Order dear, it gave the rest of Manchester a priceless gift – a future.

Without the mirrors, potted plants and sticky carpets you'd have found in most other Mancunian venues, the Haçienda, instead, was inspired by the kind of clubs then opening in New York, like the Funhouse: stripped-down, unaffected. The New York connection was a reflection of Manchester's history – at the centre of international trade routes, and as a migrant city – and the way the music community has always shared influences with a network of creative trading partners: Detroit, New York, Berlin, Glasgow. Other cities with attitude.

There's a showbiz adage that it takes years of hard work to become an overnight success, and just as bands work away in the shadows before taking centre stage, so the Haçienda had its time undiscovered. This had a precedent; in the mid-1960s, away from the pop charts, Northern Soul, the first underground club scene in Britain, developed at the Twisted Wheel on Brazennose Street, just a few hundred yards from Manchester Town Hall.

But in the late 1980s, the Madchester era, the Haçienda became the major focus for a rave new world of computer-aided dance music and acid house. Other clubs like the Thunderdome in Miles Platting, Konspiracy down by the Cathedral, the Hippodrome in Middleton, and Maximes in Wigan all had a part to play. Again, the city was awash with activity. The Madchester boom re-ignited confidence in the city and energised a new generation of hit makers, including 808 State, Happy Mondays, the Stone Roses. One of the young Madchester bands was the Inspiral Carpets who had a roadie called Noel Gallagher. His brother Liam was inspired by seeing the Stone Roses at Spike Island; six years later the two Gallagher brothers were in the biggest band in Britain, Oasis.

So the baton of creativity gets passed on. Now independent labels like Twisted Nerve, Paper and Grand Central are continuing the work started by the likes of Factory. Musicians like Badly Drawn Boy and bands like Elbow are still bringing kudos to the city.

Although the Haçienda lost its way, then closed, major DJs inspired by visits to the club have gone on to success – like Justin Robertson, the Chemical Brothers, and Sasha – and newer nights – Electric Chair, Tangled, Bugged Out, Keep it Unreal, and Tribal Sessions – have emerged at clubs like the Music Box and Sankey's Soap.

The best clubs in the city create a genuine community, contributing to Manchester's status as a music-loving city; a status sustained by a mix of influences, working class, black, Irish, Jewish, gay, art school. That's the beauty of nightlife at its best, cutting through suspicions and breaking down barriers. It's not like the world outside, all those destructive attitudes dividing communities into ghettos, tribes, niche markets.

Not all nightlife is like this, not even in a city with a highly developed music consciousness like Manchester. Plenty of activity is motivated by nothing more than the fast buck and the bottom line. But far from diluting the city's reputation as a pop culture capital, these recent developments are more likely to provoke the spirit of invention.

In a non-conformist city like Manchester, there's always a willingness to go against the grain, create something better. It might stay a secret, or it might be the next Northern Soul, the next Haçienda, or the next Badly Drawn Boy. It's not always possible to know exactly what's going on, but in Manchester you can always be sure that something is going on.

Club life

Having been into music from as far back as I can remember, becoming a DJ meant that I could go out and play my favourite tunes to other people. I was lucky enough to be introduced to the Apollo Theatre (a Sister Sledge concert) at the age of eight and I grew up with Sunset, the pirate radio station. The Manchester music scene was bound to influence my career

Danielle Moore
Manchester DJ

The Manchester Evening News Arena is Europe's largest indoor concert venue and winner of the Concert Industry Award for International Venue of the Year 2001. Hosting around 150 events annually, from major concerts to high profile sporting events, the Arena is a vital part of Manchester's leisure and entertainment culture.

>> Clockwise from top left
Lime
Taurus
The Restaurant Bar and
Grill
Simply Heathcotes

^ The string of bars,
known as Deansgate
Locks, have breathed
new life into the derelict
railway viaduct arches
beneath the old Central
Station. Their immense
popularity reflects the
casual nightlife which
embodies Manchester
in the 21st century

<< Rusholme's 'curry mile'

As night clubbers head home, an army of market traders prepare for another hectic early morning at the New Smithfield Wholesale Market

RAIN

```
w   f   t   n   w   t   r   w   r   i   c
h   a       c       r       e           u
e   l   a   h       a       a   t
n   l   h   i       t              's   n
t   l   e   e       i       h   i   t   i
h   k   s       u       i   n   n   b       a
            n   m   n   n
e   t       t       p       k       h   n
r   h   o   e   t   h   f       o   e
    e   f       h   a       o
a       m   r   n   a           w
i   y   b   e           f       m   w
        a   u   t               l   s   a
n           t               l           a
                s               n       y
```

Lemn Sissay 2002

BIOGRAPHIES **David Plowright CBE** was Editor, Programme Controller, Managing Director and Chairman of Granada Television in Manchester between 1957 and 1992. He was Chairman of the Design Panel for the Manchester Olympic Bid (1988) and Chairman of the Development Committee, Manchester City of Drama (1994) | **Phil Griffin** was born in Ancoats. He has been a radio presenter and television director. He is a regular writer for *City Life*, Manchester's listings magazine. He has written a column about Manchester buildings since 1996. He has moved seven miles in fifty years. | **John J. Parkinson-Bailey** has been teaching architectural history in the Department of History of Art & Design at the Manchester Metropolitan University for the past twenty-seven years. His most recent book, *Manchester: an architectural history*, won the 1999 Portico Prize. He lives in south Manchester with his wife and various cats. | **Sir Graham Melmoth** joined the CWS (now Co-operative Group (CWS) Limited) in 1975. He became the Group's Chief Executive in November 1996. He is non-executive Chairman of Ringway Developments p.l.c. and Chairman of the Manchester Enterprises Group. Sir Graham holds numerous executive and non-executive positions and was awarded a Knighthood in the 2002 New Year's Honours List. | **David Ward** grew up in London but moved to Northumberland at 22 and now has spent more than half his life in the north. He joined *The Guardian* in 1974 and is a news reporter covering the north west. | **Andrew Collomosse** is a freelance sports journalist based in West Yorkshire. A regular contributor to national newspapers and magazines, his sports books include *The Lion of Vienna* with Bolton Wanderers' legend Nat Lofthouse, and *Bully for you Oscar*, the life story of Lancashire cricketer Ian Austin. | **Ray King** is Manchester born and bred. Ray has been a journalist with the Manchester Evening News for almost 32 years covering industrial and political issues. For the last 16 years he has also worn the mantle of the paper's restaurant critic. | **Dave Haslam** was a DJ at the Haçienda in Manchester from 1986 to 1990 and again in 1996 and 1997. He has Dj-ed around the world including Chicago, Paris, Berlin, Detroit and 'Cream' in Liverpool. He has written two books, *Adventures on the Wheels of Steel* and *Manchester England* – voted the *Sunday Times* Pop Music Book of the Year. | **Lemn Sissay** is a 34 years old writer. His mother lives in New York and works for the United Nations. His late father was a pilot for Ethiopian Airlines. Lemn was brought up in a Lilliputian Lancashire village. Lemn spends a third of his time at home in Manchester, a third in London and the rest in Africa and America. Like Gulliver, his most inspiring thought is 'I'm bigger than this.' | **Cath Staincliffe** was brought up in Bradford and graduated from Birmingham University with a Drama degree. Moved to Manchester to work in community arts and spent the next eight years carrying out projects all over the north west in partnership with community groups. She is now writing the fifth of her Sal Kilkenny crime novels, set in Manchester, and reviews for *The Manchester Evening News* and Tangled Web. | **Jan Chlebik** enjoys photographing Manchester, a city he regards as full of contrasts. Over the years he has photographed anything and everything in and around Manchester for various clients, and has documented many changes in his hometown. He works nationally and internationally for a variety of advertising and design clients. | **Len Grant**, for the past decade he has photographed the 'new Manchester'. He has published books about the building of the MEN Arena, The Bridgewater Hall, and most recently The Lowry. He has documented Hulme's regeneration and the city's reconstruction following the 1996 bomb. He is currently photographing the Imperial War Museum North | **Paul Herrmann** has worked as a photojournalist in Manchester since 1985, concentrating on people, communities, social issues and the arts. His most recent book, *Playing with Fire*, is a photographic celebration of Manchester's Streets Ahead festival. His work appears regularly in magazines and newspapers worldwide. || ACKNOWLEDGEMENTS Thanks for advice, information and support from: **Access Cleaning** Mick Carr | **Afflecks Palace** Lynn Anderson, Stacie Nathaniel, Kelly Mills at Under your Hat, Sorted Image, Extreme Largeness, Bizantium, Ash 'n' Blotti, The Soap Cabin, Attic Fancy Dress, Kirsty at Vintage to Fetish (and especially Dorothy and Gwen) | **Al-Faisal Tandoori** | **Arc Clothing** | Duncan Kingboy Ashman | **BBC Press** Kate Butler | **Belle Vue Greyhound Track** Andy Ablett | **Choudhary Manufacturing Co.** | **City Centre Management** Gordon McKinnon | **Cosgrove Hall** Phil Gray, Amanda Thomas, AJ Read | **Crane drivers** Ian Rumney, Keith Merrick | **Eric Wright Construction** | **G.ten** Michael Pollard | **Grey Mare Lane Police Station** Inspector Peter Jones, Wyn and Margaret | Fiona Griffiths | **Hallé Orchestra** Andy Ryans | **Homes for Change** Charlie Baker | **Impact Media** Paul Patton | **Islington Mill** Bill Campbell, Adrian Beaumont | **The Jewish Museum** Don Rainger, Levi and Chana Brown, Magdalena Jones | Hugh Jolly | **Lime** Paolo Pala, David Bright | **Living Edge magazine** Colin Bannon | **Loves Saves The Day** Becky Jones, Chris Joyce and Debbie Goldsmith for her wonderful window paintings | **Marketing Manchester** Neil Jaworski, Drew Stokes, Alan Bellwood | **Manchester Art Gallery** Adam Quinn,

Kim Gowland | **Manchester City Council** Howard Bernstein, Glenice Kennedy, Richard Leese, Jane Lemon, Jill Lewis, Marina Moss, Ian McCarthy, Marilyn McGuinness, Lis Phelan, Mel Rix, Tom Russell, Bob Rutt, Jeff Staniforth, Janine Watson | **Manchester Evening News** Paul Horrocks, Peter Sharples | **Manchester Craft and Design Centre** Adrian Mason from Putti, Helen Rushworth, Linzi Ramsden, Jean Hurst, Deborah Zeldin-O'Neill, Sarah Thirwell, Collette Hazelwood and her dog | **Manchester in Bloom** | **Manchester International Convention Centre** Keith Robertson | **Manchester University Press** Matthew Frost, Alison Sparkes | **Manchester Wheelers** Tony Thurman | **MEM@2K** Mike Polaway | **J Mowlem and Co plc** Jamie Roscoe | **MIDAS** Neil Fountain | **Midland Hotel** Fabiola Renshaw, William Robinson, Adrian Hughes, Julie, Angela, Beverley and Mercedes in the Trafford Restaurant, Vicky Lucas, Jennifer Ellis, Roger Pendlebury, Paul Loftus, Kevin Scanlan, Clinton Hibbert, Michele McGowan, Sheila Hughes | Danielle Moore | All the traders at the **New Smithfield Wholesale Market** especially Elam and Hall North | **Atherley Garden Project** Dena Murphey, Bob Aspinall | **The Northern Cutter** Guy Jenkins, Jimmy Haq | **People's History Museum** Vivian Lochead Veronica Powell | Jason Queally | **Restaurant Bar and Grill** Philip Feingold, Carlos Contes | Bill Ross | **Sanam Sweet House and Restaurant** Abdul Ghaffar, Mohammed Saleem Javed | Jonathan Schofield | **Shoppers** Bethany Rogers, Roy Brandon, Beryl Kerr, Leon Noi, Anthony McMahon, Laura Clarke, Nathaniel Gulsher, Leon Bari, Zack and Azaldo, Alan and Zoë | Siemens Communications Ltd Janice Bentham | Simply Heathcotes Rino Di Stefano, Davey Aspin, Michael Curry | Lemn Sissay | **Smithfield Buildings** Simon Grennan, David Osbaldeston | Liam Spencer | **Sportcity** Scott Tacchi, Helen Collier | Nowell & Bibbi Stebbing | Katherine Stephenson | **Taurus** Iain Scott, Nico Kargas, Norbet Nowak, Peter Smith | Susannah Thompson | **True Mancunians** Sian Price, Stephen Price | **University of Manchester School of Biological Sciences** Cathy Tournier, David Barker | **Urbed** Nick Dodd | **Vertitech** Billy Sharrocks, Warren Howarth | **Waterstone's Deansgate** Jon Atkins, Dave Gledhil, Tony Grice, Dave Lovely | Mike Wilson | **Winter & Co** Steve Burdett, Julie Croydon | **Yang Sing** Harry and Gerry Yeung, Laura Salem | ...and the couple who happily walked through the Hulme park with no questions asked.

|| PICTURE CREDITS **Jan Chlebik** p1 (some), p4, p8, pp10-11, p13 (right and below), p19 (alms houses), p35, pp38-39, pp48-49, p51, p58 (below), pp66-67, p68 (left), pp74-75, p81 (left and right), p82, p87, p89, pp92-95, pp100-103, p108 (below left and right), p111, pp150-151, pp158-159 | **Len Grant** cover, spine (below), p1 (some), p14, pp16-17, p18 (top), p19 (except alms houses), p20, pp22-25, p27, p28 (top and below left), p29, pp32-33, p44, p59, pp62-63, p70, p72, p83, p96 (below), p98, pp104-107, p110, pp114-115, p116 (top), p117, p121 (below), p122, p126 (top left), pp130-133, pp135-137, p139 (top right), p144, pp146-147, pp154-155, p156 | **Paul Herrmann** spine (top), p1 (some), pp2-3, p7, p9, p12 (except below left), p13 (top), p18 (below left), p28 (below centre), pp40-41, p42 (top and below), p43 (top), p46, p47 (except below), pp52-53, p54 (below), p55, p58 (top, Bill and Ben © BBC/Ben Productions), pp60-61, p68 (below), p69 (right), p76 (below five except 'crowd'), pp77-79, pp90-91, p96 (top), p97, p108 (top), p113 (below), pp118-119, p121 (top and right), p125, p126 (top right), p128, p129 (except below), p134, p138, p139 (except top right), p142 (top), p143, p152 (below) p153 (below left and right) | **Ian Lawson** p6, pp30-31, p42 (centre), p47 (below), p64, pp84-85, p112, p126 (below left and right), p127, p129 (below), p152 (top), p153 (top) | **picturesofmanchester.com/Len Grant** p12 (below left), p18 (below right), p26, p28 (below right), p43 (below left and right), p50, p54, p65, p69 (below), p73, p76 (top five except 'moustache'), p80, p81 (top and below), p86, p120, p124, p142 (below) | **MEM@2K** pp36-37 Daniel DeGiovanni p36 (top), Della Batchelor p36 (below), Lorna Ruskin p37 (top), Mike Poloway p38 (below) | **Gten photography and design** pp56-57 | **Clive Totman** p68 (top) | **Marketing Manchester** p88, p96, p109 | **picturesofmanchester.com/Howard Barlow** p113 (diver) | **picturesofmanchester.com/Will Cross/Skycam** p116 | **picturesofmanchester.com/Patrick Henry** pp140-141 | **Jon Super** pp148-149 | **Ben Stebbing** p160 || PRODUCTION DETAILS **Photographic co-ordination** Len Grant | **Design** AW assisted by ZR @ www.axisgraphicdesign.co.uk | **Fonts** Solex (healines) and Scala (text) | **Print** Clifford Press, Coventry | **Paper stock** text and dustjacket HannoArt 170 & 150 gsm respectively produced by Sappi, endpapers Colorit Sapphire Blue 160 gsm produced by StoraEnso | **Binding materials** trade edition bound in Wibalin, and luxury edition bound and slipcased in Brillianta Calandre from Winter & Co |

Clinamen Press extents its gratitude to **James McNaughton Paper Group Ltd** for paper kindly supplied and to **Winter & Co** for their assistance in the publication of this volume. And finally... **Special thanks to Manchester City Council, commissioners of** *The Mancunian Way.*

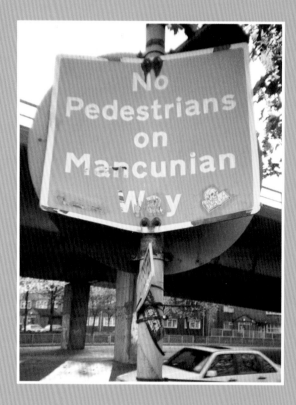

The Mancunian Way
© 2002 Clinamen Press Ltd
Photography © individual photographers
Text © individual contributors

Published by
Clinamen Press Ltd
4 Potato Wharf
Castlefield
Manchester
M3 4NB

www.clinamen.co.uk

ISBN: 1903083818 hardback
ISBN: 1903083826 hardback with slipcase

First Edition

1 3 5 7 9 8 6 4 2